# Green Cleaning with Vinegar

# Vinegar Benefits, Cleaning Tips and Vinegar Uses

By

**Claire Hammond**

**Copyright 2015**

# Table of Contents

Introduction……………………………..4

Living Room……………………………12

Kitchen…………………………………..24

Bathroom………………………………..42

Laundry…………………………………51

References………………………………62

## Introduction to Cleaning with Vinegar

Vinegar is probably that one condiment no kit hen would be able to live without, and for good reason! A ide from being a condiment, vinegar can also be used as a cleaner, polish, bleach, disinfectant, insecticide, drain opener, and deodorizer. But what exactly is the secret behind vinegar's multitasking powers?

The secret lies in acetic acid which is the activ e ingredient in vinegar. Recent clinical research shows hat acetic acid can effectively kill some forms of disease-causing bacteria. According to a report published in *i Bio*, the online open-access journal of the American Socie y for Microbiology, researchers discovered that a 6% solut on of acetic acid is powerful enough to kill mycobacterium even highly drug-resistant *Mycobacterium tuberculosis* (the bacterium that causes tuberculosis). The report theref re concluded that acetic acid has the potential to serve as an effective but non-toxic and affordable disinfectant against the said microbes. While chlorine bleach effectively disinfects TB cultures and clinical samples, it is highly toxic and corrosive. The cost of other effective commercial disinfectants is extremely prohibitive, making it impossible for laboratories and healthcare facilities in developing countries (where majority of TB cases originate) to use them.

If acetic acid can be powerful enough to kill highly drug-resistant bacteria, then common sense dictates that ordinary table vinegar, which usually contains 5% acetic acid, can effectively get rid of many common household bacteria, such as viruses and fungi. Moreover, since vinegar does not contain poisonous and corrosive ingredients, it can be counted on to safely clean most household surfaces, such as:

- Countertops

- Stainless steel

- Tiles

- Windows

- Carpets and rugs

- Hardwood

- Leather

- Upholstery

- Stovetops

- Cutting boards (both wood and plastic)

- Microwave oven

- Washing machine

- Plastic ware

- Glassware

- China

- Crystal

- Porcelain

- Ceramic

- Silverware

- Brassware

- Copperware

The following pages contain ideas on how to use vinegar to clean your home. But before you start cleaning, always keep the following safety precautions in mind:

- Always test <u>any</u> cleaning solution on a hidden area first. This will ensure that you will not encounter any undesired surprises!

- Before cleaning an electrical appliance (e.g., microwave oven, refrigerator, etc.), make sure that the appliance is switched off and unplugged.

- Never use vinegar or any acidic cleaner on marble, limestone or granite surfaces, it will erode the stone.

- Never combine vinegar and chlorine bleach. Mixing bleach with an acid will produce chlorine gas, which can be fatal if inhaled.

## Living Room

Some people would rather put up with dirty venetian blinds than go through the difficult and time-consuming process of cleaning each slat individually. The good news is that you don't have to be one of them! Vinegar can make the job of cleaning venetian blinds less torturous.

Combine equal parts hot tap water and white vinegar. Put on a white cotton glove and dampen the fingers in the mixture. You can then proceed to clean your venetian blinds by lightly sliding your gloved fingers over each slat.

Want to keep your piano free from dirty fingerprints and other stains?

Mix ½ cup vinegar and 2 cups water. Wet a soft cloth with the solution, wring the cloth until there's no more water left in it and then gently wipe each key. Use another cloth to wipe the keys dry. Leave the keyboard uncovered for 24 hours to completely

remove the scent of vinegar from it.

Water rings can make even the most beautiful piece of

wood furniture look unsightly. Before you decide to have

your water-stained coffee table professionally repaired, or,

worse, throw it out, try this simple trick first:

> Mix equal parts olive oil and vinegar. Using a soft
>
> cloth, apply the solution to the water ring. When
>
> applying the solution, see to it that you follow the
>
> direction of the wood's grain to prevent cross-grain
>
> scratches. Use another soft cloth to wipe off excess
>
> solution (this will also make the furniture look
>
> shiny).

Noticeable scratches on your wooden tabletop? They may

appear hard to correct, but vinegar can actually make them

appear less obvious.

In a small jar, combine some refined or cider vinegar and iodine. Dip a small artist's brush into the mixture and paint the solution over the scratch.

But what if water rings appear on your leather furniture? Pat some undiluted white vinegar on them with a sponge. Before you know it, those water rings on your leather couch will be history, and you can save yourself a few bucks in repair costs!

Do you want your leather sofa or easy chair to look like it did the day you bought it? Vinegar can help you restore it to its former glory!

Combine equal parts white vinegar and boiled linseed oil. Using a spray bottle, spray the solution on your leather furniture. Spread the solution evenly over the whole area with a soft cloth. Wait for a few minutes to allow the solution to settle into the leather, and then wipe off excess solution with another soft cloth.

Heavy foot traffic will definitely leave your carpets and rugs dirty and worn. Make your rugs and carpets look clean and new again by brushing them with a clean push broom doused with a mixture of 1 cup white vinegar and a gallon, (3.7 liters), of water. There's no need to rinse your carpet or rug afterwards.

Do you have mildew forming on the bottom of your rugs and carpets? Spray undiluted white vinegar at the back of your rug or carpet, and watch the mildew disappear!

Stubborn stains on rugs and carpets? Remove them with these:

> For light stains, dissolve 2 tablespoons salt in ½ cup white vinegar. Rub the solution on the stain and let it dry. Vacuum the carpet afterwards.

To treat larger or darker stains, add 2 tablespoons borax to the aforementioned solution. Treat stains in the same manner.

For really tough stains and deep-seated dirt, combine 1 tablespoon vinegar with 1 tablespoon cornstarch. Mix them well until they form a paste. Using a dry cloth, rub the paste onto the stain and let it set for 2 days. Vacuum the carpet or rug afterwards.

Need and on-the-go carpet and rug stain remover? Fill a spray bottle with 1 part vinegar and 5 parts water. Fill another spray bottle with 5 parts water and 1 part non-foaming ammonia. Spray the vinegar solution on the carpet or rug stain. Wait for a few minutes and then blot the stain carefully with a clean, dry cloth. Spray and blot using the ammonia solution. Repeat until the stain is completely removed.

Furniture polish or wax is intended to protect and shine

wood and leather furniture. But prolonged usage of

furniture polish or wax can cause buildup, dulling the finish

of your wood coffee table or leather couch. Moreover

polish or wax buildup can attract dirt and dust, making your

table or couch look dirty. Here are simple tricks to get rid

of polish or wax buildup:

For wood furniture, mix equal parts vinegar and water. Wet

a soft cloth with the solution, wring the cloth until there's

no more water left in it and then gently wipe away the wax

or polish. When wiping, make sure to follow the direction

of the wood's grain to prevent cross-grain scratches. Use

another soft cloth to wipe the area dry.

For leather furniture, combine ¼ cup vinegar and ½ cup

water. Dip a soft cloth into the solution and then wipe away

the wax or polish. Wipe the area dry using another soft

cloth.

**Kitchen**

A clogged drain is not only inconvenient; it can also  e

expensive and potentially dangerous. A plumber's se  /ices

can cost you hundreds of dollars. Commercial drain

cleaners can be expensive and ineffective. Commerci  l

drain cleaners are caustic, which means they contain

chemical substances that damage pipes and pose heal  h

hazards. Fortunately, there's a simple way for you to

unclog your drain without sacrificing your pipes, you

wallet, and your health.

Using a funnel, pour ½ cup baking soda and 1  cup

vinegar directly into your drain (the solution  ill

cause foaming in your drain). As soon as the

foaming stops, pour some hot water into your  lrain.

Pour cold water into your drain after five min  tes.

Bonus: The said formula not only unclogs dra  ıs; it

also deodorizes them, baking soda has a
deodorizing effect.

If your entire kitchen reeks of smoke, don't worry it happens to everyone! Eliminate the smoky odor by placing a bowl of white or cider vinegar in the area where the odor is strongest. This will remove the odor in less than a day. Would you like the smoky odor to be gone faster? Moisten a piece of cloth with full-strength vinegar and wave it around your kitchen for a few minutes.

Are you having a hard time removing grease stains from your kitchen? The solution is simple!

Combine equal parts white vinegar and water. Dip a cloth in the solution and wipe the grease off. Want to boost your dishwashing detergent's grease-fighting capabilities? Mix 3-4 tablespoons white vinegar with your dishwashing detergent.

Do you hold your breath every time you open your child's lunchbox, because it smells of week-old tuna no matter how many times you wash it? Leave a slice of white bread soaked in vinegar in the lunchbox overnight. The smell should be gone the next morning. Your child will definitely thank you for it!

Here's a quick and easy way to clean your microwave:

> In a glass bowl, mix together ¼ cup vinegar and 1 cup water. Place the bowl inside the microwave and heat the mixture for five minutes on the highest setting. Once the mixture cools down, use it to wipe away stains and splatters on the microwave's interior.

Aside from baking soda, vinegar is also an effective and safe cleanser for your refrigerator.

> In a small bucket, mix together equal parts water and white vinegar. Using a sponge or a soft cloth, wipe the solution on the refrigerator's interior and

exterior. Mildew growth in your refrigerator? Pour some full-strength vinegar on a soft cloth and then wipe it on the affected area. Do the same thing to remove dust and grime at the top of your refrigerator. Don't forget to leave a box of baking soda in your refrigerator after cleaning up to keep it smelling fresh.

Preventing food-borne illnesses requires more than just washing hands, you also need to properly clean your cutting board and butcher-block countertop! Never use water and dishwashing detergent on them. Dishwashing detergent can weaken surface wood fibers. Instead, wipe your cutting board and butcher-block countertop with undiluted white vinegar after each use. The acidic nature of vinegar renders it an excellent disinfectant, effectively killing harmful bacteria such as E. coli, Salmonella, and Staphylococcus. Smelly cutting board and butcher-block countertop? Sprinkle some baking soda over them and then spray on full-strength vinegar. Wait for five to ten minutes (the solution will cause foaming), then rinse using a cloth soaked in clean cold water.

Want to make your silverware look new without using an expensive and toxic silver cleaner?

Combine ½ cup white vinegar and 2 tablespoons baking soda. Soak your silverware (pure silver cutlery, candlesticks, rings, necklaces, bracelets, etc.) in the solution for 2-3 hours. Afterwards, rinse them in cold water and thoroughly wipe them dry with a soft cloth.

But what about your brass and copper items?

Combine equal parts white vinegar and salt, or vinegar and baking soda. Mix them together until they form a paste (if you use vinegar and baking soda, wait for the foam to subside before using).

Rub the paste on your brassware and copperware with a paper towel or a soft cloth until the discoloration is gone. Rinse thoroughly with cool water and dry with a soft cloth.

Are you at a loss as to how to clean your delicate china, crystal and glassware? Try these:

The next time you run your dishwasher, pour ¼ cup vinegar to its rinse cycle. Your glassware will come out gleaming.

Hard water stains ruining your drinking glasses? Boil a mixture of equal parts white vinegar and water (use undiluted white vinegar for more stubborn hard water stains). Soak your glasses in the mixture for 15-30 minutes. Scrub stains with a bottle brush and rinse clean.

Wash your delicate crystal glasses by adding 2 tablespoons vinegar to your dishwasher. Then rinse them in a solution of 3 parts warm water and 1 part vinegar. Air-dry your glasses afterwards.

Wash delicate crystal and fine china by gently
dunking them in a basin of warm water mixed with
1 cup vinegar. Air-dry afterwards.

Stubborn coffee stains on your china dishes and
teacups? Mix together equal parts vinegar and salt.
Scrub this solution on your china dishes and
teacups. Rinse them with warm water afterwards.

Does your coffee always taste weak or bitter? It
probably means that you need to clean your
coffeemaker.

Pour 2 cups white vinegar and 1 cup water into the
decanter. Put a filter in your coffeemaker. Pour the
solution into your coffeemaker's water chamber.
Switch on the coffeemaker and run a full brew
cycle. Discard the filter and the solution. Rinse the
decanter. Repeat the process, but this time, use cold
water, this will ensure that the water and vinegar

solution has been completely washed out of your coffeemaker.

You can use the above recipe in your single serve coffee maker as well!

Moths and other bugs invading your cupboard and pantry? Don't even think about reaching for that bottle of commercial insecticide. Commercial insecticides may be effective in killing bugs, but they emit noxious fumes that are very dangerous to your health. Here's a safer alternative:

In a small bowl, combine 1 ½ cups apple cider vinegar and a few drops of dishwashing liquid. Leave the bowl in your cupboard or pantry for a week, the solution will attract the bugs, causing them to fall into the bowl and drown. After a week, clean out your cupboard or pantry with 1 liter of water mixed with dishwashing detergent or 2 cups baking soda. Dispose all wheat products (flour, bread, noodles, pasta, pastries, etc.) and wash the surfaces of canned goods before returning them. Once Fruit flies invade your kitchen they are very hard to remove! Here's a simple but effective trap for fruit flies:

Fill an old jar at least halfway with apple cider vinegar. Punch a couple of holes in the lid, screw it back on and leave the bottle in the area infested by fruit flies.

**Bathroom**

Mildew stains in your bathroom?

Mix together equal parts white vinegar and water. Using a soft cloth, wipe the solution on the stained area. For heavier mildew concentrations, use undiluted white vinegar.

Water spots and soap scum can make even the most elegant porcelain look old and dingy. Make your porcelain sinks and bathtubs look new again with these simple tips:

Restore your sink and bathtub's shine by scrubbing them with undiluted white vinegar. Rinse with clean cold water afterwards.

Stubborn hard water stains on your bathtub? Fill your bathtub with hot tap water mixed with 3 cups white vinegar (make sure that the solution fills up over the stains). Let it soak for 4 hours. Afterwards, drain the water and scrub off the stains.

Whitening your grout need not be time-consuming and

expensive. All you have to do is to dip an old toothbrush in

white vinegar and start scrubbing away. It's that simple!

Want to remove annoying water spots from your shower

doors? Combine ½ cup white vinegar, 1 cup ammonia, ¼

cup baking soda and 1 gallon, 3.7 liters, warm water. Dip a

cloth into the mixture and wipe them down. You'll have

sparkling clean shower doors in no time.

It is very important that you regularly clean your rinse cup.

Since a rinse cup accumulates water over time, it's a

potential breeding for disease-causing germs and bacteria.

Clean your rinse cup once a week by filling it with equal

parts white vinegar and water, or

undiluted white vinegar, and then let the solution sit overnight. Rinse thoroughly with cold water before using.

Have you noticed that you're getting less water from your shower than before? A likely culprit behind is a clogged showerhead. Years of mineral deposits in the water can clog your showerhead, blocking the normal flow of water coming from it. You can wash away blockages and mineral deposits from your showerhead with these simple tips:

If your showerhead is removable (and made of metal), put it in 1 quart (1 liter) boiling water with 1/2 cup distilled vinegar for 10 minutes. If your showerhead is made of plastic, use hot (not boiling) water. The blockages should be gone after a 10-minute soak.

But what if your showerhead is non-removable? Fill a small plastic bag halfway with full-strength vinegar and tape it over your showerhead. Let it sit for 1 hour, then remove the plastic bag and wipe away remaining traces of vinegar from your showerhead.

Dirt and grime can accumulate in the tracks of shower doors over time. This problem can be solved by filling the tracks of your shower doors with 2 cups undiluted white vinegar and letting the vinegar sit for 3-5 hours, (for really dirty tracks, use undiluted white vinegar that has been heated in a microwave oven for 30 seconds). Flush away the gunk afterwards by pouring hot water over the tracks. Use a small scrub brush or an old toothbrush to get rid of extra stubborn gunk.

You can keep your toilet clean and smelling fresh without using expensive store-bought cleaners! All you have to do is pour 2 cups of full-strength white vinegar into your toilet bowl and let the vinegar sit overnight before flushing. Make this a weekly habit and before you know it, that ugly water ring, the dark brown stain that typically appears just above the water level, will be erased as well.

Your shower and toilet are not the only bathroom fixtures you can clean with vinegar! Full-strength white vinegar poured onto a soft cloth can be used to polish chrome faucets, towel racks, bathroom mirrors and doorknobs. Is your toothbrush holder grimy, full of bacteria and toothpaste residue? Wipe the openings with cotton swabs dampened with undiluted white vinegar.

**Laundry**

Running colors in the wash are a waste of time and money.
Prevent running colors with this simple precaution: Before
washing your new clothes for the first time, soak them in a
few cups of vinegar for 10-15 minutes. Running colors will
never be a problem for you again!

Want to throw out your plastic shower curtain because it
has ugly mildew stains on it? Before you do that, try this
simple tip first: Toss your shower curtain and some dirty
towels into your washing machine. Pour a solution of ½
cup laundry detergent and ½ cup baking soda to the load.
Wash the load in warm water on your machine's regular
cycle. Add 1 cup white vinegar to the first rinse. Before
your machine goes into the spin cycle, remove the shower
curtain and hang it to drip-dry.

Is your washing machine making your clothes dirtier? Dirt,
grime and soap scum can accumulate in your washing

machine over time, rendering your clothes dirty no matter how many times you wash them. Hence, it's extremely important that you regularly clean out your washing machine. Just follow these steps:

Pour 2 cups full-strength vinegar into your washing machine.

Run your machine through a full cycle (without any clothes or detergent). If your machine is really dirty, fill it with very hot water mixed with 2 gallons (7.5 liters) vinegar and let the agitator run for 8-10 minutes.

Turn off your machine and let the solution stand overnight. The next morning, drain the basin and run your machine through a full cycle (this time, use clean water).

Chlorine bleach is great for killing germs, but it isn't exactly safe for cloth diapers and your baby's skin. Relax! You don't have to make your baby put up with germ-laden cloth diapers. When washing cloth diapers, just add 1 cup of undiluted vinegar to the first rinse. Not only will vinegar disinfect your cloth diapers; it will also help rinse out the detergent from your cloth diapers faster, vinegar is acidic, so it dissipates the bubbles and the detergent therefore rinses out faster.

Want your laundry to come out soft and fresh-smelling without spending a fortune on fabric-softening liquids and sheets? Here are some tips:

Mix together 1 gallon white vinegar and 30-40 drops of essential oil. Don't forget to shake well before use.

When rinsing small or average loads, pour ½ cup of the solution into the rinse cycle. Just increase the amount for larger loads.

To make dryer sheets, cut a large piece of cotton cloth into smaller sections, (there's no need to buy new cloth—you can use old t-shirts or linen).

31

In a small bowl, mix together ½ cup of vinegar and 8 drops essential oil. Moisten the cloths with the solution. Store in an airtight container. To use, simply take out a sheet from the container, wring out excess solution back into the container and toss into the dryer. Once your clothes are already dry, just return the sheet back into the container for future use. Also, make sure that you regularly remoisten your sheets with the aforementioned solution.

Lint and static on your clothes? Get rid of them by pouring 1 cup of vinegar into the last rinse. It's that simple and cheap!

Stains are really a pain. Not only is the process of taking them out very time-consuming, you'll also have to spend a fortune on detergents, bleaches and spray, some of which don't even work! The good news is that vinegar can effectively remove even the toughest stains on your clothes, minus the expensive price tag!

Here are some suggestions:

Are your white socks dingy? Brighten your white socks with this simple tip: In a large pot, boil 1 ½ quarts (1.5 liters) tap water mixed with 1 cup vinegar. Pour the solution into a bucket and soak your dingy socks in the former overnight. Wash your socks the next day.

Unless you love wearing yellow-tinted clothing, here's a simple way to restore your yellowed garments: Soak them overnight in a mixture of 12 parts warm water to 1 part vinegar. Wash your clothes the next day.

Treat water-soluble stains (beer, fruit juices, coffee, tea and vomit) on washable cotton blends by blotting them with a cloth or towel moistened with full-strength white vinegar. Wash as usual afterwards. For large stains, soak the stained clothing overnight in a solution of 3 parts vinegar to 1 part cold water. Wash as usual the next morning.

Tougher stains such as blood, cola, hair dye, wine and ketchup on washable cotton blends should be treated within 24 hours. Using a sponge, apply undiluted vinegar to the stain and then wash as usual afterwards. If the stain is really severe, add 1-2 cups of full-strength vinegar to the wash cycle as well.

Want to throw out a garment because of older, set-in stains? Before you do that, try this first: Add 3 tablespoons white vinegar and 2 tablespoons liquid detergent to 1 quart (1 liter) warm water. Blot the solution into the stain and then wash the garment as usual.

Perspiration stains can be unsightly and embarrassing! Get rid of them with this quick and easy trick: Make a paste of 2 parts white vinegar to 3 parts baking soda. Rub the paste onto the stain and let it sit for half an hour. Wash as usual. Don't have time to make a paste? Pour undiluted vinegar directly onto the stain and rub into the fabric before washing as usual.

# References

95+ Household Uses for Vinegar. (2015). *Reader's Digest.*

Retrieved January 24, 2015, from

http://www.rd.com/home/150-household-uses-for-

vinegar/

Active Ingredient in Vinegar Can Effectively Kill

Mycobacteria. (2014, February 25). *News-*

*Medical.net.* Retrieved February 2, 2015, from

http://www.news-

medical.net/news/20140225/Active-ingredient-in-

vinegar-can-effectively-kill-mycobacteria.aspx

Helmenstine, A.M. (2014, November 29). Mixing Bleach

and Vinegar: Why You Shouldn't Mix

Bleach and Vinegar and Why People Do It

Anyway. *About.com.* Retrieved February 2, 2015,

from

http://chemistry.about.com/od/toxicchemicals/a/Mixing-Bleach-And-Vinegar.htm

Heloise. (2015). 9 Cleaners You Can Make Yourself. *Good Housekeeping*. Retrieved February 2,

2015, from

http://www.goodhousekeeping.com/home/cleaning-organizing/make-at-home-cleaners

Taylor, N. (2014). Vinegar: (Almost) the Only Cleaner You'll Ever Need. *The New Homemarker*. Retrieved February 2, 2015, from

http://www.thenewhomemaker.com/cleanorg/vinegar.html

Printed in Great Britain
by Amazon

30577846R00022